STEP YOUR GAME UP

WITH 5 SIMPLE DAILY
ROUTINE SALES EXERCISES
THAT WILL STRENGTHEN
YOUR SELLING SKILLS

AN AUTOMOTIVE SALES GUIDE TO SUCCESS

STEP YOUR GAME UP

WITH 5 SIMPLE DAILY
ROUTINE SALES EXERCISES
THAT WILL STRENGTHEN
YOUR SELLING SKILLS

XULON PRESS

ROGER LOVE

Xulon Press
2301 Lucien Way #415
Maitland, FL 32751
407.339.4217
www.xulonpress.com

© 2021 by Roger Love

All rights reserved solely by the author. The author
guarantees all contents are original and do not infringe
upon the legal rights of any other person or work. No
part of this book may be reproduced in any form without
the permission of the author. The views expressed in
this book are not necessarily those of the publisher.

Paperback ISBN-13: 978-1-6312-9846-2

CONGRATULATIONS

Welcome to the World of Automotive Sales! So, now that you are working for a dealership, I am quite sure you have a ton of questions and concerns each day you walk into your dealership. *The one concern you should have right now is sustaining a solid career in sales.*

I want to share one bit of advice with you that I received when I first got into the dealership business. The first general manager I ever worked for, Alan Marzano, told me, "Get in one place and stay there; then everyone will know where to find you." That my friend, stuck with me my entire career because it helped me to establish roots; also, for people to know who I was and what I could do for their car problems. I was committed and I worked in that one car dealership for nearly twenty years, selling lots of cars; many of them were the easiest sales I ever made. Why? Because people knew who I was and what I *could do*. I developed lots of relationships with people, as you should always know that selling is relational. So, I want to advise you to plant yourself in the very dealership you are in and do not uproot under any circumstances if possible.

Part of the problem with new salespeople like your-self is that they do not stay in one place long. When things get tough, I want you to get tougher and face it, learn from it and grow from it. Do not be like the average salesperson in this business, *who* when things are not going their way, they just pick *up* and run for refuge to another dealership or another job. Just remember if you run from trouble once, you will do it again! I want you to learn from this booklet and learn to stay planted like a tree. So, if you know anything about trees, then let's look at palm trees. For example, palm trees, when planted, their roots will begin to make a strong effort to reach out horizontally from the tree house where they stabilize and anchor into the soil. So, when storms, such as the hurricanes in Florida, come, the palm trees are

_____

IN THE AUTOMOTIVE SALES INDUSTRY, YOU WILL NEED TO DO THE SAME AND PLANT YOURSELF; BEGIN TO WATER YOURSELF WITH KNOWLEDGE, SELLING SKILLS, CONFIDENCE, AND ORGANIZATIONAL SKILLS; HAVE THE SPIRIT OF AN ENTREPRENEUR, ALONG WITH THE HEART OF A CHAMPION

_____

so strong at the trunk that the trees can withstand most storms and hurricanes. [1]

In the automotive sales industry, you will need to do the same and plant yourself; begin to water yourself with knowledge, selling skills, confidence, and organizational skills; have the spirit of an entrepreneur, along with the heart of a champion, to keep your head in the game and begin to plant your roots all the way down to the bedrock of your knowledge.

Inside this booklet, I want you to take full advantage of everything that I am going to teach you, which will include the five principles you will need to have to step your game up and to become a true professional in this business. I want you to begin earning $75,000 per year and up, which is the earning of the title "True Sales Professional." My goal is not to promise you that I can make you a Rockstar in the business, but it is to give you the necessary skills needed to be great in this profession. So, use this booklet as the foundation to build a career like a skyscraper that will stand tall in your dealership every month. Ready to make some real money? Let's go!

Be The Greatest Version of You,
Roger Love

---

[1] Teo Spengler, "Palm Tree Facts," *Hunker,* November 30, 2017, https://www.hunker.com/12568030/do-palm-tree-roots-grow-as-big-asthe-palm-tree.

TABLE OF CONTENTS

ACKNOWLEDGEMENTS

Thank you, God, for allowing me to display and use my talents for the betterment of this world. I am so grateful for the love you have shown me.

I want to thank my wife Tosha who has been my number one cheerleader from day one, my wife, business partner and best friend. I cannot fail to mention the love and support of our three kids Jalen, Jalante and True. And, not to forget you either, Karolyne. I want to thank my longtime friend and brother Atif Jabli for his help and support. Nick Jones thanks for the support. Reecie and Dale Craft thank you guys for your continued contributions of love and support throughout my life. Cannot forget my car biz family, John Barrett, man thank you for teaching me to show up and get after it everyday. Brad Mugg, thanks brother for giving me the opportunity to be great. Lastly, I want to thank Mr. Bob Rohrman for teaching me so many things about the business, believing in my vision to someday obtain my own store, and the biggest one is to never give up. Thank you shouts to my pastors, Wayne "Coach" Gordon and Carey Casey for being a beacon of light in my life.

Also, thank you to all my family and friends, the people who have impacted my life, even still to this day.

WHAT DO YOU ULTIMATELY WANT?

I have interviewed thousands of prospective sales-people for nearly two decades, and in these inter-views, one of the most important questions I would ask these candidates is this: "What do you ultimately want from the car business?" Many times, most of the young people would look at me somewhat puzzled and respond by saying one of two things: one is "I do not know" and the other is "money." When they say money, I then would ask another question: "How much do you want to make in a year?" Some have the audacity to reply $35,000 to $40,000 per year. This is where most answers are, which is so low and it gives me a perspec-tive of their expectations, which are also low.

Usually when candidates respond to the money question with such a low range, I look at them and ask, "Did you apply for the right job? I have lots of porters at my store making the money you are wanting, not to mention I am looking to replace a few current sales-people who seemed to have lowered their standards and are pacing the $35,000 to $40,000 range. I do not want them here and if those are your expectations as a new hire candidate, then I probably do not want you either." Then you have the people who really do not know what they want, which that, my friend, scares me right away and totally turns me off. I cannot find interest in someone who is coming into a sales interview and does not have a clue as to what they want.

You have older candidates who know what they want, and that is to be able to pay their bills and get out of debt. However, when I typically ask the older candidates, they just want to make around $40,000 to $50,000, which is not the way to get out of debt; it would simply be just enough to get by. You see, when I ask, "What do you ultimately want out of the car business?" I get high expectations from candidates, and sometimes I have the occasional candidate who comes in and answers with high expectations of themselves. They want to make big money $65,000-$70,000 range, which is okay. I then asked them, "are you willing to take the necessary measures to do whatever it takes to make the big bucks?" Most of the time the answer is yes and then I usually tell them the expectations of the dealership's salespeople, as well the amount of time plus effort it would take to make the big bucks. Usually you can see the signs of commitment in their eyes or the lack of in their eyes.

You probably ask yourself, *why are you telling me all this, Roger?* Well, it is quite simple. If you are getting into this business, you had better know what exactly it is you want, along with having an idea of what it will take to get to the things you ultimately desire to have.

Listen people, sales are one of the highest paid professions in the world. Why? Because the sky's the limit and there is nothing stopping you but you! I want you to be in the automotive sales industry and ultimately know what it is you want, but also have a strong commitment to do what it takes to get there. So many people come into a job and this job, automotive sales profession, and are clueless when it comes to knowing what they want. If you know the number one thing that you desire to have, then you will be motivated to do what it takes

IF YOU KNOW THE NUMBER ONE THING THAT YOU DESIRE TO HAVE, THEN YOU WILL BE MOTIVATED TO DO WHAT IT TAKES TO REACH, OR EVEN EXCEED THAT DESIRED THING. YOU MUST HAVE EXPECTATIONS BECAUSE THEY SET THE TABLE FOR YOUR GOALS, YOUR MOTIVATION, AND YOUR DRIVE TO BE SUCCESSFUL.

to reach, or even exceed *that desired thing*. You must have expectations because *they* set the table for your goals, your motivation, and your drive to be successful. I want you to complete the exercise right now in the spaces below. Write down what it is *that* you ultimately want from selling cars.

REVIEW EXERCISE

What do you ultimately want from selling cars?

_____

_____

What do you believe it is that you will need to have in order to be successful in achieving your desires from the car business?

_____

_____

_____

Studies show that fifty percent of goals written down are achieved.[2] Do you have your goals written down currently? _____ If not, why not?

_____

_____

_____

Write down your goals below. They do not have to be all car business- related. Personal goals are perfectly okay. Besides, this is your very own booklet in which you have invested in for yourself.

_____

_____

_____

*Tell someone who is close to you about your goals and have them become your accountability partner. Goals shared with someone *that is* special to you are more

---

[2] *Engagement Multiplier*, "New Year's Employee Engagement Strategy: Set Realistic Goals," January 9, 2019, https://www.engagementmultiplier.com/blog/new-years-employeeengagement-strategy-set-realistic-goals/.

likely to be achieved too! You will need someone to hold you accountable.

STUDENT OF THE GAME

All the greats in any industry were great at what they did simply because they understood their industry and the people that are in their industry, as well as the people *who paved the way for them in their particular industry*. This means they studied history of the business, both past and present. What I mean by this is that they studied the business, learning the history and origin of the business? Some say it is not important; I say it is so important. The better you understand where certain things came from, the better you will appreciate what it is you do; also, the more you are aware of the current trends and current events, the better you will be. I will give you an example: Have you ever gone some place to buy something and the sales associate you were dealing with could not answer your questions? Perhaps you have had a great salesperson on the other hand, who was sharp, entertaining, and dynamic, giving lots of information for you to make wise decisions? Then you bought the product because they made it simple. You get my point?

Step Your Game Up

I want to give you a few tips on what I mean by **Student of The Game.** For instance right now, as I am writing and designing this booklet, we are in the middle of an economic shutdown-lockdown due to the Coronavirus (COVID19) and dealerships, as well as salespeople, now all have adapted to home deliveries, using on-line videos, social media, and video email, plus other digital outlets to do business now. So, if you want to be great in the car business, then you had better study the business and adjust to the current times or get left behind.

A GREAT DEAL OF SALESPEOPLE WHO ARE NEW IN THE BUSINESS NEVER STUDY OUTSIDE OF WORK. THEY ALSO NEVER PRACTICE, DRILL, OR REHEARSE THEIR SELLING SKILLS. SO, THEY NEVER LEARN THE BASICS OF SELLING, RELYING INSTEAD ON THEIR SALES MANAGERS AND HOPING THEY WILL HELP THEM TO SELL CARS.

A great deal of salespeople who are new in the business never study outside of work. They also never practice, drill, or rehearse their selling skills. So, they never learn the basics of selling, relying instead on their sales managers and hoping they will help them to sell cars. This crutch of relying on sales managers is dangerous and leads to a couple of things that can happen to you as new sales-people, which could run you right out of the business. They, of course, have one of several scenarios that run them out of the business: they get fired for not selling enough cars; they quit because they are frustrated due to lack of skills; or they blame their sales managers for not helping them to sell enough cars and not making enough gross profit to make money of course.

As a student of the business, you should be doing the following all day, every day.

1.) **Learn how people think and process things in their minds. It really is not that hard just to sit and watch people who shop,** whether they are at a mall, a department store or even a restau-rant. Just watch them, from their mannerisms to the way husbands and wives communicate with each other in public. You should just sit silently somewhere near by them and observe their eye contact, listen to the tone and inflection of their voices. Now when it comes down to how people think, just ask friends and relatives about what they like and dislike about buying cars or just shopping in general.

2.) **Just listen to them and do this on a regular basis until you become very observant in watching**

———————

THE PHRASE "I SUGGEST" OR "I RECOMMEND YOU TRY THE ATLANTIC SALMON. IT IS ONE OF OUR MOST POPULAR DISHES" IS MOST HELPFUL. YOU CAN LEARN TO DO THE SAME IN LEARNING TO ASK THE RIGHT QUESTIONS OF CUSTOMERS SO THAT YOU WILL KNOW WHAT TO RECOMMEND OR SUGGEST FOR YOUR CUSTOMER TO DO WHEN THEY MAY BE UNCERTAIN.

———————

and listening to what people say and do when shopping or out to eat. I believe if you really want to be good at both, observe a waiter the next time you are at a fancy restaurant. Watch how they interact and communicate with the customer. Listen to them how they tell the history of the restaurant, how they help to clarify what the customer wants so they get it right. Now, most great waiters will always have a favorite or something they highly recommend when the perplexed customer comes in and does not have a clue what to order off the menu. The phrase "I suggest" or "I recommend you try the Atlantic Salmon. It is one of our most popular dishes" is most helpful. You can learn to do the same in learning to ask the right questions of customers so that you will know what to recommend or suggest for your customer to do when they may be uncertain. This will show strength in your selling skills and deem you as a professional who is confidently in control; all because you have studied and prepared yourself for situations such as helping the *indecisive* customer. It will always make you look great and sharp when you can direct the customer by saying, "Most of my customers usually go with this color or trim level," and you simply say, "Here's what I suggest you go with." This shows me that a salesperson has done his/her homework and has studied *their* customers.

3.) **Now another area I suggest you work on is using your voice in the sense of tone and inflection.** What do I mean by this? For example, there are going to be times *when* you need to have some excitement and enthusiasm in your voice. The customers come to the dealership and they are greeted by you for the first time — this is when you want to have some enthusiasm in your voice to welcome them to the dealership. Show *them* that you are excited *that* they are there, it also shows them that you are very interested in serving them. ***Customers love a warm greeting; now remember, don't be too***

overexcited because sometimes you will need to tone it down to match the personality of the customers, so you do not turn them off or make them feel awkward . Now, on the other hand, you will need to be able to lower your tone when you are presenting numbers to customers, just to let them know you have worked out a great deal for them. In doing that, you will need to know how to sit down with them, look them square in the eyes, and say, "I have worked on your behalf to get you some awesome numbers." Now, you are using your voice to gain their undivided attention. *There are other skillsets in which you will need to work on, so I want you to study and study like never before to be one of the greatest students when it comes to learning how to sell cars. Also, never stop learning and never stop being a student*. The late great Kobe Bryant was a student of the game of basketball. Even after he retired, he took on coaching young girls right up until his untimely death in 2020. So never stop learning, never stop growing in the business because of new technology and unfortunate *sometimes an act of nature, case in point*, the Coronavirus shutdown-lockdown that is currently *having an adverse effect on the* automotive industry, *as we speak*. Learning new technology and new skills will always add value to you as a sales professional.

4.) Lastly, learn to practice patience with your customers and do not be pushy with them. Among other things, check your attitude. You will need to make sure your mindset is in the right place because your customers can feel your energy. The energy generated by your attitude does not lie.

_____

AMONG OTHER THINGS, CHECK YOUR ATTITUDE. YOU WILL NEED TO MAKE SURE YOUR MINDSET IS IN THE RIGHT PLACE BECAUSE YOUR CUSTOMERS CAN FEEL YOUR ENERGY. THE ENERGY GENERATED BY YOUR ATTITUDE DOES NOT LIE.

_____

NUMBERS GAME

I f you have not heard this yet, then you will *hear it now*; the car business is a numbers game. Earlier I told you that last year in a Cox Automotive study, dealerships reported an eighty percent turnover rate with their salespeople in 2019.[3] This basically means that a vast majority of the people in the car business left their dealerships in this study; *they quit the business or left for* another dealership. Remember the advice I got from my first general manager? Therefore, you must learn the business, understand the business, and that starts with the numbers. In another study for example, Accenture surveyed ten thousand customers in 2019 and discovered that car buyers are showing an average between thirteen and fifteen hours of shopping before deciding

---

[3] Cox Automotive, *2019 Dealership Staffing Study: Engage your People and Optimize your Greatest Asset,* PDF file (Atlanta: Cox Automotive, 2019), https://d2n8sg27e5659d.cloudfront.net/wpcontent/uploads/2019/07/2019-Dealership-Staffing-Study-Final-.pdf.

to buy.[4] Autotrader reported that fifty-nine percent of buyers spend time online researching their next car purchase.[5] Before leaving home, seventy-eight percent of customers have already decided to buy a vehicle. The first ninety days in the car business are crucial because, again, you read and understand the turnover numbers; a great majority of salespeople that quit or are fired happen during these first three months in the business.

As you can see, not only do you need to be a student of the business, but you also need to understand that this business is all about knowing and understanding the numbers. Here is another statistic for you: Only seventy-seven percent of consumers are satisfied with their salesperson, leaving only seventy-six percent of all people who are satisfied with their total dealership experience. This is an important one: Seventy-one percent of people say they bought from a dealership only

---

[4] Cox Automotive, *2019 Car Buyer Journey,* PDF File (Atlanta: Cox Automotive, 2019), https://d36fcomet71j7t.cloudfront.net/oem/wpcontent/uploads/2019/12/2019-Car-Buyer-Journey-Study.pdf.

[5] *V12,* "25 Amazing Statistics on how Consumers Shop for Cars," June 12, 2019, https://v12data.com/blog/25-amazing-statistics-on-how-consumersshop-for-cars/.

because they liked and trusted their salesperson.[6] Still, to this day, over fifty-five percent of customers leave a dealership without ever being offered a test drive. Also, in an Autotrader study, sixty-one percent of customers' first contact with a dealership is when they walk into the showroom for the first time, which this will change after COVID-19 for sure. These statistics are important because a part of most salespeople's pay is tied into what customers think of their service and treatment, which is called a Customer Survey Index (CSI). You will need to understand how that can truly affect your pay as a new salesperson, plus me telling you this should bring more awareness to discovering why customer service will be important to your career.

There are so many other numbers to go over; however, I just wanted to give you some insight as to why I say that this is a numbers business. Check this out: fifty percent of customers say that they bought their car right on the spot because they got a great presentation and demonstration on the car they were interested in from their salesperson.[7] When it comes down to shopping, there are two things that stand out to me: one,

---

[6] Jeff Kershner, "Dealer Showroom Floor Sales Statistics and Percentages," *Dealer Refresh,* August 7, 2008, https://www.dealerrefresh.com/dealershowroom-floor-sales-statistics-and-percentages/.

[7] Ibid

seventy-eight percent of customers, according to Auto Trader, used third-party sites to shop, while fifty-seven percent preferred to use dealership websites when it came to dealership website usage.[8] Customers also said the purchases took an average of three hours to complete the process.[9] When it comes to dislikes, eighty-seven percent of Americans dislike something about buying cars[10] and sixty-one percent feel that they are being taken advantage of while they are there in the dealership.[11] Another forty-nine percent feel like they were tricked into buying features they did not agree with during their purchasing process.[12] Now millennials, for instance, when it comes to technology, seventy percent cite technology and infotainment as must-haves in their next vehicle purchase.[13]

---

[8] *V12*,"25 Amazing Statistics on how Consumers Shop for Cars."

[9] Cox Automotive, *2019 Car Buyer Journey.*

[10] *V12*,"25 Amazing Statistics on how Consumers Shop for Cars."

[11] *Beepi, Inc.*, "Study: Americans Feel Taken Advantage of at the Car Dealership," July 21, 2016, https://www.prnewswire.com/news-releases/studyamericans-feel-taken-advantage-of-at-the-car-dealership-300301866.html.

[12] *V12*,"25 Amazing Statistics on how Consumers Shop for Cars."

[13] Ibid.

I want you to get the gist of understanding numbers not just in a sense for negotiating purposes, but to know what the law of averages are so that you will know what you need to know in order to be sharp. Being sharp, in a sense, is that you will work harder than the salesperson at the next dealership to win a customer's business. Sales is also about knowing how to differentiate yourself from the competition and understanding the numbers of this business will help because the numbers do not lie; they represent true facts. When you have facts, you have knowledge. Of course, knowledge increases your confidence and the desire to do better. You want to be good in this business: study the numbers every chance you get, as they are right in the palm of your hand with our current smartphone technology.

"SALES IS ALSO KNOWING HOW TO DIFFERENTIATE YOURSELF FROM THE COMPETITON AND UNDERSTANDING THE NUMBERS OF THE BUSINESS WILL HELP BECAUSE THE NUMBERS DO NOT LIE; THEY REPRESENT TRUE FACTS."

REVIEW EXERCISE

What are three things that stood out to you in learning about the numbers side of the business?

_____

_____

What were the two things I said that stood out to me in studying the numbers?

_____

_____

In looking at the sales turnover percentage in the number section, what does it tell you about the importance of your first ninety days in the business?

_____

_____

_____

FIVE DAILY ACTIVITIES YOU MUST DO TO BE SUCCESSFUL IN THE CAR BUSINESS

A s I stated earlier in this booklet, the chances of you making it in the car business all comes down to what you do in your first ninety days. Now if you are at a typical dealership, your training may consist of three to five days of training from the management staff, which involves you learning a few selling skills on your own and then, after that, you are left on your own to study the product. During this time frame, you are trying to learn the business in the sense of taking a "crash course" on how to sell cars, along with the pressure of getting certified by your

> *AS I STATED EARLIER IN THIS BOOKLET, THE CHANCES OF YOU MAKING IT IN THE CAR BUSINESS ALL COMES DOWN TO WHAT YOU DO IN YOUR FIRST NINETY DAYS.*

manufacturer's product knowledge, in which you cram to just get it done. This is done in a sense to get management off your back so you can be released to the sales floor to sell cars, leaving many of you totally unprepared. Deep down inside, you and your sales managers know that you may not be ready.

> *DEEP DOWN INSIDE, YOU AND YOUR SALES MANAGERS KNOW THAT YOU MAY NOT BE READY.*

Now you might be paired up to work with a veteran salesperson who is drooling over you to take half of your deal because you lack knowledge and skills, leaving you *unprepared and possibly not* learning anything at all. This, in turn, only allows frustration to set in. Now the sales manager is on you because you don't have enough deals worked or cars sold, so your confidence is now shot down a notch. You may even be thinking about abandoning ship and leaving because it is not what you expected. Now, I just gave you a scenario of what could be happening to you right now, or it may go through your mind as you read this booklet. Perhaps you have not been in this place yet in your new career, which is good for you. However, I wanted to give some insight to what happens in most dealerships to new hires and no one seems to care. Well, I do care!

So, I want to share with you five things you must consistently do daily for the first ninety days in your sales career. This will be the planting of your roots, just as I explained to you about the palm trees in Florida. I want you to get planted and deeply rooted in the basic skills that are required to sell successfully planting yourself in one place This is so when hurricanes come your way, you can withstand the strong winds and survive the storms of the business. I want to be clear with you: This booklet is not a solution to saving your career. It is an option to show you the way to sustaining a solid foundation to selling and an option for you to make a commitment in being more successful over mediocrity. I want you to strongly make a commitment to completing these five daily activities. Now is the time to "Step Your Game Up!"

REVIEW EXERCISE

Why are the first ninety days so important to you being new in the car business?

_____

_____

FIVE SALES EXERCISES TO STRENGTHEN YOUR SELLING SKILLS

Practice, Drill, Rehearse (PDR): I want you to understand something. The *best* way to *Perfect and become skillful* at selling is to practice using those skills as much as possible every day, doing drills that will enhance your muscle memory and rehearsing it as if you were auditioning for a Broadway play or a movie role. An amateur athlete must practice on his/her skillsets *daily* and sometimes they *advance* to the collegiate level, but very few make it professionally in sports. So *this is* why I told you that eighty percent of sales-

> *IF YOU ARE GOING TO MAKE IT AND THRIVE IN THIS BUSINESS, THEN YOU HAD BETTER BEGIN TO SHARPEN YOUR SELLING SKILLS."*

people quit the business, or *they are* fired, all because of poor performance.

If you are going to make it and thrive in this business, then you had better begin to sharpen your selling skills." Let's take the Road to The Sale", "Ten Steps to The Sale" or whatever your dealership may label it. *You must learn each and every one of those steps, without question.* So, in order to do that, you will have practice doing them daily to get familiar with them, do you agree? Now let's take the greeting for example. You are going to have to get used to greeting people in a professional way like, "Welcome to ABC Motors. My name is and you are?" You must practice with a partner at work, go home and drill this in your head by writing it out on paper. Maybe you begin to do this by recording it with your phone and begin reviewing it repeatedly; then rehearsing it with someone at home or work.

Now you are going to need to put your skills to the test every day with real customers. The more customers you can get in front of and greet, the stronger you will become. Yeah, you might stumble over the words a couple times, but you will get it. Now you will need to also learn the rest of the road to the sale, according to your dealership's standards. The more you *practice*, the better you will become and eventually it will sound smooth like a true professional. Now typically you should have this mastered in a week or two. There are other skills and techniques you will have to learn, but

THERE ARE OTHER SKILLS AND TECHNIQUES YOU WILL HAVE TO LEARN, BUT THE WHOLE IDEA I WANT YOU TO GET FROM THIS IS THAT EVERYTHING YOUR MANAGERS OR TRAINERS TEACH YOU IS UP TO YOU TO DO THEM EVERY DAY AND MASTER THEM TO PERFECTION.

the whole idea I want you to get from this is that everything your managers or trainers teach you is up to you to do them every day and master them to perfection. Every opportunity you get, practice, drill, and rehearse *your skills to the point that it becomes so natural that you do not e*ven have to think about it anymore because it becomes second nature.

Your level of mastery will kick in, and that will *be sustained by* good habits and rituals that must be done every day, especially in your first ninety days as a new salesperson. So, remember *daily* **practice + drill +rehearse = mastery.** Your goal is to become a Master at every skill that you are taught, from the greeting to investigating, to doing a walk around the demonstration/presentation, to negotiating skills to learn timing on when and how to ask closing questions. It is your responsibility to learn and perform like a professional. This will take time. Be patient but be diligent and eager to

THIS WILL TAKE TIME. BE PATIENT BUT BE DILIGENT AND EAGER TO LEARN WHAT IT TAKES TO BECOME GREAT AT SELLING CARS.

HOWEVER YOU NAME IT, NO MATTER THE BRAND OR HOW ADVANCED A CRM MAY BE, MOST SALESPEOPLE, ESPECIALLY NEW SALESPEOPLE, FAIL TO USE IT FOR TWO REASONS. **FEAR** *AND* **LAZINESS** *ARE REASONS THAT SALESPEOPLE GET SOLD INTO BECOMING AN AVERAGE SALESPERSON BUT ARE SOON REPLACED FOR LACK OF SALES PERFORMANCE.*

learn what it takes to become great at selling cars. **Practice, Drill, Rehearse, and Master** *Now, you are on course* to "Step Your Game Up!"

1.)   **Master Your CRM System:** If you desire to be really great at selling cars for a living, then I can tell you that you will need to master the CRM System your dealership uses, which is the second key to building a solid foundation. Let's define CRM for those of you who do not know the meaning of these initials. Customer Relationship Manager is a tool used by companies, such as your dealership, to perform a combination of strategies, best practices, analysis of customer interaction, and the use of customer data throughout the sales cycle of the lifetime of that customer. The use of collected data is to improve customer service relationships. In short, it is the best friend and secretary of a data tracker that a salesperson could have. However you name it, no matter the brand or how advanced a CRM may be, most salespeople, especially new sales-people, fail to use it for two reasons. **Fear** and **laziness** are reasons that salespeople get sold into becoming *an average* salesperson but are soon replaced for lack of sales performance. You look at the best and the worst salespeople, along with your average salespeople. They all learn just enough to get management off their backs.

Whenever salespeople decide to learn, they will just simply take the time out to master the CRM system. They would sell far more cars and build a solid repeat-and-referral business, *and* most *important* of all staying connected with their customers. I have witnessed far too many sales-people short-cutting (not following the sales process) and not learning the proper use of their CRM, all because they feel it slows them down; when, in fact, it speeds it up. There are dealer-ships out there paying, on average, $6,000 to $10,000 per month for CRM tools but a vast majority of new hires, and old veteran salespeople too, struggle with using it; all because of the lack of desire to use it and the fear of losing a sale. Little do they know they will eventually lose a sale anyway because most dealerships usually make it a house rule that in order to claim a customer, you must protect yourself by putting them in the CRM and *you will* have seventy-two hours, at the most, of recent contact to split or to justify that the person is your customer. That only goes so far though.

Here is what I want you to do as a new salesperson. First, take the time to learn the basics of the CRM system that your dealership is using.

Really learn the basic functions of the CRM, such as how to enter a customer into the system: how to fill in

REALLY LEARN THE BASIC FUNCTIONS OF THE CRM, SUCH AS HOW TO ENTER A CUSTOMER INTO THE SYSTEM: HOW TO FILL IN ALL THE CUSTOMER INFORMATION, YEAR, MAKE AND MODEL OF THE CAR, THE STOCK NUMBER, THE TRADE IF THERE IS ONE, PAYOFF, ETC. IT IS IMPORTANT THAT YOU GET EFFICIENT IN DOING THIS.

all the customer information, year, make and model of the car, the stock number, the trade if there is one, payoff, etc. It is important that you get efficient in doing this. Do not call a veteran salesperson or sales manager to keep doing it for you because you will never learn. Learn how to print out the information, learn how to complete the credit application, or complete the insurance forms and the entire deal jacket. How you do this is the same way I just told you in the first of the five ways to "Step Your Game Up." This too will require you to practice, drill, and rehearse over and over. Take the tutorials that are available, seriously. Heck call the vendor of the CRM company or get a salesperson who is knowledgeable with the tool or even a sales manager to explain something that may be hindering you. There's nothing wrong with asking for help. Your CRM will more likely be smartphone accessible and will make your life so much easier, but you must master the functions of your CRM in order to be successful. Take it from me; I have seen many salespeople fail simply because they refuse to take the time to learn the CRM.

YOUR MOST IMPORTANT TOOL WILL BE YOUR CRM

Your most important tool will be your CRM, for it will help you to master follow-up, video messaging, text messaging, social media marketing to your contacts, and, of course, phone and email contact. If you want to sell and be successful, then you must master staying in constant contact with your customer. I do not care what line of the selling business you are in; the way to follow up and stay in contact with your customer will be one of the most effective keys to selling. You can record notes, keep records of your contact information, contact your customer for service, birthdays, purchase anniversaries, and opportunities for repeat-and-referral business by setting reminders. It will only happen if you master the CRM system properly. So, I want you to come in everyday to practice, drill, rehearse, and master the art of communicating with your customer through your dealership's CRM.

Mastering communication with your customer will help you to "Step Your Game Up" and build a solid customer base for yourself.

Here is a bonus piece of advice for you: I want you to take every person in your phone that can buy a car and place them in your CRM and make them the foundation of building a customer base.

You can start with an email, phone call, text or a social media message to them to let them know what you are doing now. In a Facebook study forty-nine percent of users shared their auto-related content with their networks. While seventy-eight percent of users found social media useful when deciding on buying a new automobile.[14] If your name is not coming up in car conversations amongst family and friends...shame on you! Family and friends will be the easiest sale you will ever make, because they already like and trust you. Begin to master your dealership's CRM with what's in your smartphone.

REVIEW EXERCISE

Why is the CRM important in selling cars?

_____

_____

---

[14] *Facebook IQ*, "Understanding the Auto-Buying Journey of the Connected Consumer," December 3, 2018. https://www.facebook.com/business/news/insights/understanding-the-auto-buying-journey-of-the-connected-consumer.

What does a CRM help you do?

_____

_____

What are two key skills the CRM can help you to develop?

_____

_____

What do the initials "CRM" spell out?

_____

3.) **Active Communication Skills:** Your selling skills are one thing for you to learn and master. Now your active communication skills are what will win you over with a lot of customers in your career. As you already know, communication is the key to staying in contact with your customers, understanding what their wants and needs are in order to meet their needs. To put yourself in a position to win, you will need to enhance your active communication skills. You may be wondering what

_____

NOW YOUR ACTIVE COMMUNICATION SKILLS ARE WHAT WILL WIN YOU OVER WITH A LOT OF CUSTOMERS IN YOUR CAREER.

_____

exactly active communication is. Well, active communication is using a selected skillset to engage someone in detailed communication with you. For example, when you are meeting a customer for the first time, you learn the person's name and begin to use it through your presentation by asking questions that will involve him or her to answer. Best way to actively communicate with someone is to ask him or her *"either-or"* questions. Such as, "Are you seeking a light color or dark color?" "Have either of you seen our newly redesigned showroom?"

These questions will engage the customers and get them to tell you more about their desires for their next new car or the information you will need to make a great sales presentation. Let's take another example: the customers leave the dealership and you want to keep them engaged. You might send them a text with a GIF or video of the car they just drove, telling them a little more about the car that could be a bonus. Perhaps you email the customer and place an eye-catching

> *BEST WAY TO ACTIVELY COMMUNICATE WITH SOMEONE IS TO ASK HIM OR HER "EITHER-OR" QUESTIONS.*

YOU MUST BECOME SO ACTIVE WITH YOUR COMMUNICATION THAT IT MAKES THE CUSTOMER COMFORTABLE TO ENGAGE IN A CONTINUED CONVERSATION WITH YOU.

statement in the opening message such as, "I am so excited about your next new car, look what I did." You must develop a great rapport with the customers while they are in your presence and then **"WOW"** them even more after they leave your presence. That's right be impressive. Use both names of the husband and wife or all the names of the party who came to the dealership to impress them. You must become so active with your communication that it makes the customer comfortable to engage in a continued conversation with you. More importantly, you must get them to like you. As I stated earlier that people buy from you because they like and trust you, this will allow you to discover the best way to communicate with them.

Active communication will take time and effort, like anything else you will learn to do in this business, but you will have to be committed to learning how to communicate with customers actively, which will improve your earnings in this business. It is your duty to keep your customers engaged. I want you to practice learning your customers' names at the greeting and continue using their names throughout the duration of their visit. Then learn how to engage them even more after they leave, whether they buy a car or not. Now one thing that will be key in active communication is learning to listen twice as much as you talk. The dollars are in the detail and listening is key because when you repeat or remind them of something they said, they will be aware you were listening to them, which is a great form of active communication. A great deal of customers does not buy from salespeople or dealerships who do not listen to their wants and needs.

Other keys to active communication are things such as your smile, eye contact, the excitement level in your voice and body language that will tell it all. So, work to make sure these things are on point with lots of practice, drilling, and rehearsing until you master them. Also, you want a customer to remember you, so be the last face he or she sees at your dealership, i.e., you walk out to thank them before they leave out with their new car or you walk them to their car as they are leaving if they do not buy the car. Customers very rarely remember their salespeople; be so active with your communication skills that you will stand out from the competition.

REVIEW EXERCISE

What is active communication?

_____

_____

What can active communication do for you?

_____

_____

4.) **Shameless Self-Promotion:** When you enter the world of sales and you are working strictly on commission; this means if you do not sell you do not get paid. Not selling, not getting paid, is not what the job is all about and you deserve to get paid. Now the reason most people in the car business become a part of the eighty percent who have failed, as I discussed earlier, is because they were too afraid to be successful. They did not know how to be successful; they were not properly trained to be successful, or they did not listen and were too arrogant, which led to their dismissal. The one thing a great majority did not do or were not taught to do is how to market and promote them- selves as sales professionals. As a sales professional in the car business who works on commissions, you must learn how to do **"Shameless Self Promotion."**

You must look at the car business like this: Your dealership will market and adver-

NOW THE REASON MOST PEOPLE IN THE CAR BUSINESS BECOME A PART OF THE EIGHTY PERCENT WHO HAVE FAILED, AS I DISCUSSED EARLIER, IS BECAUSE THEY WERE TOO AFRAID TO BE SUCCESSFUL.

tise itself all day every day on the television, the radio, on social media and other digital outlets. The dealership you work for will sometimes spend hundreds of thousand dollars, and some even into the millions, each year to advertise to their market. They are and will always be telling you who they are, what they sell, what services they offer, what's on sale, and what you can buy for a special deal on a current day. Now I am not telling you to go out and spend some insane money to market yourself. Just look at it like this; if no one knows you sell cars, then you are probably not going to have a chance at selling many cars. However, if you begin to see yourself as a business professional and you want to discover a way to let more people know what you do for a living, then you will need to begin to discover ways to position and market yourself to your marketplace. Your marketplace is the people who you know, besides they already like, trust, and respect you.

_____

Look at it like this: In your smartphone, you have on average, like most people, at least 250 to 300 contacts in your phone and you may even know how many of

JUST LOOK AT IT LIKE THIS; IF NO ONE KNOWS YOU SELL CARS, THEN YOU ARE PROBABLY NOT GOING TO HAVE A CHANCE AT SELLING MANY CARS.

_____

them own an automobile or two, right? So, your first marketplace is located right in the palm of your hand and you need to let everyone know what you do, whether they drive the brand of car you sell or not. Eventually, if you shamelessly promote yourself enough to the people in your phone, they will let someone know what you do if the car conversation should come up or they will contact you about purchasing a car. For example, I want you to do this after reading this section. Send a text blast to everyone you know in your phone, letting them know that "I am a sales professional, and this is where I am working. Should you have any car sales needs, I am a phone call away." Perhaps you really decide to "Step Your Game Up"

IF YOU SHAMELESSLY PROMOTE YOURSELF ENOUGH TO THE PEOPLE IN YOUR PHONE, THEY WILL LET SOMEONE KNOW WHAT YOU DO IF THE CAR CONVERSATION SHOULD COME UP OR THEY WILL CONTACT YOU ABOUT PURCHASING A CAR.

and create a digital flyer to advertise to all your social media contacts, as well by email, about who you are and what you do. Then I recommend you take it even further and let some of the social media groups you belong to in on what it is you do. Post on your social media sites two or three times per day; go live and talk about yourself and your product on the regular. You have got to blow your own horn and blow it loud so they will hear you.

Please do not forget about things such as the Facebook Marketplace or Instagram where you can place used cars on display. Currently, I believe you can upload only two per day, so why not do it? If you sell one car off promoting yourself, is it worth it? Absolutely!

PEOPLE WOULD FLOCK TO ME AFTER CHURCH, SEEKING INFORMATION. THAT SOON TURNED INTO SEVENTEEN TO TWENTY CARS PER YEAR AND THEY WERE SOME OF THE EASIEST DEALS I HAD EVER DONE.

I can remember when I was in the business back in Chicago. I would let the people in my church know what it was I was doing, since I had retired from teaching high school. I went from selling one car to one of my best friends to selling my pastor and his family cars. Then soon, after my pastor started telling people to go see

Roger if you want a Honda or a car right during his Sunday sermons. People would flock to me after church, seeking information. That soon turned into seventeen to twenty cars per year and they were some of the easiest deals I had ever done. I would pull into my church parking lot on Sundays and see nothing but Hondas throughout a great majority of the parking lot. It gave me a great feeling because my shameless self-promotion took off for me.

What I am telling you to do? I want you to tell it to the world in which you know that you are a car-selling professional and if they have needs, you can assist them. We used to label this prospecting; I now call it "shameless self-promotion." I want you to right now start marketing yourself, as the cost is really nothing unless you choose to invest in yourself; of course, you can do that too. You want to make it big in the car business, so promote yourself and build relationships with people and be proud of what you do. Do not be ashamed as if you are a drug dealer or doing something that is looked down on. Who cares about the myths and noise that people make about the shady car salespeople? It's all about how you present yourself. I want you to write in some answers to the questions below for you to have in order to develop a strong understanding of shameless self-promotion.

REVIEW EXERCISE

What is your definition of the term shameless self-promotion?

_____

_____

_____

What was another name I used to describe shameless self- promotion?

_____

What are three ways you can shamelessly promote yourself to sell more cars?

_____

_____

_____

5.) **Entrepreneur Mindset:** I want you to understand something about the world of an automotive sales professional. You are working for yourself. In other words, you are a business within a business, and you must conduct yourself as such. Yes, you do receive a paycheck from your dealership, which is based on your ability to create enough gross profit to receive a percentage of the proceeds. Now with that said, I want you to say this to yourself right now: "I am an entrepreneur and I am the CEO of ME, Myself, and I, Incorporated." You are basically incorporated as a "business within a business," simply because you are paid totally on your sales performance, which will require you to have the mindset of an entrepreneur.

"I AM AN ENTREPRENEUR AND I AM THE CEO OF ME, MYSELF, AND I, INCORPORATED." YOU ARE BASICALLY INCORPORATED AS A "BUSINESS WITHIN A BUSINESS," SIMPLY BECAUSE YOU ARE PAID TOTALLY ON YOUR SALES PERFORMANCE

The definition of "entrepreneur," according to the dictionary, is "a person who starts a business and is willing to risk loss in order to make money" or "one who organizes, manages, and assumes the risks of a business or enterprise."[15] Note the keywords business and risk.

In the car business, you must have a mindset like an entrepreneur and understand that you are, in fact, taking risks because sometimes you will make money and sometimes you will lose money. My sales manager, Larry Jensen, once said to me, "Roger, in this business sometimes you eat steak and sometimes you eat lima beans, but you take everything else in between." For example, most dealerships will have what they call a "mini-deal," which could pay you on a deal that does not make you any money at all because the gross is in the negative. Then you would receive on average between $100 to $150 dollars, which I look at as a loss to a salesperson. by the time you take taxes and other dealership

---

[15] *Dictionary.com*, "Entrepreneur," https://www.dictionary.com/browse/entrepreneur

fees, what you may have is next to nothing. Now let's say you sell a vehicle and the gross profit is $2000 after the dealership's holdback/pack has been removed and your percentage for example, is 25 percent, which means you would earn $500 before taxes. This is a financial gain for you. Now you will have ups and downs in this business, which is a given in the beginning for any business. There are always risks involved. Let's say, for example, a customer leaves your dealership and buys from your competitor. Then this would be a total loss to you because you truly earned nothing.

I am trying to prepare your mind for, the fact, that you must have a hustler's mentality, which is what entrepreneurism is all about. The other words used to describe an entrepreneur are "a go-getter, a businessman or businesswoman, a wheel-and-dealer, merchant,

I AM TRYING TO PREPARE YOUR MIND FOR, THE FACT, THAT YOU MUST HAVE A HUSTLER'S MENTALITY

promoter, mover-and-shaker," just to name a few. I want you to understand that as long as you're selling a product, you had better be making some moves to strengthen your skills, promote your business, follow up with customers, become dynamic, and be great at presenting an ideal to make this business venture well worth your time. There's no time to sit around huddling up, especially with average or negative salespeople who complain all day about the dealership's advertising not working for them or about the weather and economy. You are not on a salary and even if your dealership offers you a salary, you will not make it off that money alone. I am sure if you have not yet, you will meet those people who attempt to live off lower standards of income sooner or later, so stay away from them!

You want to separate yourself from them. I would be so bold as to wear a suit and tie or a nice business suit every day, unless it was unbearably hot outside, to distinguish yourself from the rest of the dealership's sales staff. One thing for sure, your customers will notice your professional appearance and they will remember you too. It may seem small to many, but remember you are a businessperson functioning within a business, and nothing happens until something is sold.

REVIEW EXERCISE

What is an entrepreneur?

_____

_____

_____

What are things that entrepreneurs are willing to do?

_____

_____

_____

*Now I have given you the true foundation of what it will take to build a successful career as an automotive sales professional. This will require total commitment from you, which will set you up for a lifetime of opportunities that will better your life and the special people who are close to you and may even depend on you. I would not be telling you this if I did not experience the fruits of my labor from working hard in the automotive industry. Now your success is totally up to you, but it will all be based on what you do in the first ninety days. I want you to keep this booklet with you and review it, write plenty of notes in it, study the business: be determined to be successful selling cars. This, my friends, is all about your mindset; this business is eighty percent mental. You Must believe in yourself. Now it's time to "Step Your Game Up!'

BIBLIOGRAPHY

Beepi, Inc. "Study: Americans Feel Taken Advantage of at the Car Dealership." July 21, 2016. https://www.prnewswire.com/news-releases/studyamericans-feel-taken-advantage-of-at-the-car-dealership-300301866.html.

Cox Automotive. *2019 Car Buyer Journey.* PDF File. Atlanta: Cox Automotive, 2019. https://d36fcomet71j7t.cloudfront.net/oem/wpcontent/uploads/2019/12/2019-Car-Buyer-Journey-Study.pdf.

Cox Automotive. *2019 Dealership Staffing Study: Engage your People and Optimize your Greatest Asset.* PDF file. Atlanta: Cox Automotive, 2019. https://d2n8sg27e5659d.cloudfront.net/wpcontent/uploads/2019/07/2019-Dealership-Staffing-Study-Final-.pdf.

Dictionary.com. "Entrepreneur." https://www.dictionary.com/browse/entrepreneur.

Engagement Multiplier. "New Year's Employee Engagement Strategy: Set Realistic Goals." January

9, 2019. https://www.engagementmultiplier.com/ blog/new-years-employeeengagement-strate- gy-set-realistic-goals/.

Facebook IQ. "Understanding the Auto-Buying Journey of the Connected Consumer." December 3, 2018. https://www.facebook.com/business/news/ insights/understanding-the-auto-buying-jour- ney-of-the-connected-consumer.

Harvey, Brooks. "Here's What You Need to Know About Millennial Car Shopping habits." *Autoguide,* November 7, 2016. https://www.autoguide.com/ autonews/2016/11/here-s-what-you-need-to- know-about-millennial-carshopping-habits.html.

Kershner, Jeff. "Dealer Showroom Floor Sales Statistics and Percentages."*Dealer Refresh,* August 7, 2008. https://www.dealerrefresh.com/dealershow- room-floor-sales-statistics-and-percentages/.

Spengler, Teo. "Palm Tree Facts." *Hunker,*November 30, 2017. https://www.hunker.com/12568030/ do-palm-tree-roots-grow-as-big-asthe-palm-tree

V12."25 Amazing Statistics on how Consumers Shop for Cars." June 12, 2019. https://v12data.com/ blog/25-amazing-statistics-on-how-consumers- shop-for-cars/